SALES TRAINING BASICS

THIRD EDITION

Elwood N. Chapman

> **WARNING**
>
> **FAILURE TO LEARN THESE
> SELLING TECHNIQUES
> COULD BE HAZARDOUS
> TO YOUR WEALTH.**

A FIFTY-MINUTE™ SERIES BOOK

CRISP PUBLICATIONS, INC.
Menlo Park, California

SALES TRAINING BASICS
A PRIMER FOR THOSE NEW TO SELLING
THIRD EDITION

Elwood N. Chapman

CREDITS
Editor: **Michael Crisp**
Layout and Composition: **Interface Studio**
Cover Design: **Carol Harris**
Artwork: **Ralph Mapson**

Copyright © 1986, 1988, 1992 by Crisp Publications, Inc.
Printed in the United States of America

English language Crisp books are distributed worldwide. Our major international distributors include:

CANADA: Reid Publishing Ltd., Box 69559—109 Thomas St., Oakville, Ontario, Canada L6J 7R4. TEL: (905) 842-4428, FAX: (905) 842-9327

Raincoast Books Distribution Ltd., 112 East 3rd Avenue, Vancouver, British Columbia, Canada V5T 1C8. TEL: (604) 873-6581, FAX: (604) 874-2711

AUSTRALIA: Career Builders, P.O. Box 1051, Springwood, Brisbane, Queensland, Australia 4127. TEL: 841-1061, FAX: 841-1580

NEW ZEALAND: Career Builders, P.O. Box 571, Manurewa, Auckland, New Zealand. TEL: 266-5276, FAX: 266-4152

JAPAN: Phoenix Associates Co., Mizuho Bldg. 2-12-2, Kami Osaki, Shinagawa-Ku, Tokyo 141, Japan. TEL: 3-443-7231, FAX: 3-443-7640

Selected Crisp titles are also available in other languages. Contact International Rights Manager Suzanne Kelly at (415) 323-6100 for more information.

Library of Congress Catalog Card Number 91-77081
Chapman, Elwood N.
Sales Training Basics
ISBN 1-56052-119-8

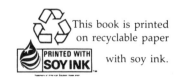

This book is printed on recyclable paper with soy ink.

TO THE READER

When you finish this brief book you will understand many aspects of professional selling. What you learn, and the changes you make after completing this program, are far more important than the time it takes to finish. *Do not read so fast that you miss something.*

Selling should be fun and exciting. You should think of it as a game and enjoy the process in much the same way you do with a favorite sport or pastime. But selling is also a profession. Like a sport, it is possible to learn principles and methods, and then practice the skills you have acquired until you become proficient. The best way to become successful at selling is to enjoy it fully, but also learn all you can about the process. It is the combination of a positive attitude and the skills you acquire that will help you become a more productive salesperson.

Good luck!

Elwood N. Chapman

Elwood N. Chapman

P.S. The person who provided this book wants you to enjoy it now, and keep it for future reference. If you have a problem as you proceed, return to this individual for help.

ABOUT THIS BOOK

SALES TRAINING BASICS is not like most books. It stands out from other self-help books in an important way. It's not a book to read, it's a book to *use.* The unique "self-paced" format of this book and the many worksheets encourage a reader to get involved and try some new ideas immediately.

This book will provide an awareness and understanding of the basics of selling. Using the simple yet sound techniques presented can help any person new to sales better understand the concepts of what is involved in the selling process.

SALES TRAINING BASICS can be used effectively in a number of ways. Here are some possibilities:

—**Self Study.** Because the book is self-instructional, all that is needed is a quiet place, and some time. By completing the activities and exercises, a reader should receive practical ideas about how to handle a sales situation regardless of experience.

—**Workshops and Seminars.** The book is ideal for assigned reading prior to a workshop or seminar. With the basics in hand, the quality of the participation will improve, and more time can be spent on concept extensions and applications. SALES TRAINING BASICS is also effective when it is distributed at the beginning of a session and the participants "work through" the contents.

—**Remote Location Training.** Books can be sent to those not able to attend "home office" training sessions.

There are several other possibilities that depend on the objectives, program or ideas of the user.

One thing for sure, even after it has been read, this book will be looked at—and thought about—again and again.

CONTENTS

INVITATION

The voluntary contract on the facing page is designed to help you become the best possible salesperson within a period of 30 days. To use it effectively, have your supervisor (or another manager) agree to a meeting to evaluate your progress as a salesperson. This meeting will give you an opportunity to ask questions about your techniques and personal progress and openly discuss what you can do to improve even more in the future.

Do ask your superior to set a date, designate a time and location, and sign the contract. Establishing this goal and arranging for future assistance is a smart thing to do. You will become the primary beneficiary!

VOLUNTARY
CONTRACT*

I, _____ , hereby agree
  (Your Name)

to meet with the individual designated below within

thirty days to discuss my progress toward incorporating the

techniques and ideas presented in this program. The purpose

of this meeting will be to *review* areas of strength and

establish action steps for areas where improvement may

still be required.

_____
Signature

I agree to meet with the above individual on

_____
Month   *Date*   *Time*

at the following location.

_____

_____
Signature

*This agreement can be initiated either by you or your superior.
Its purpose is to motivate you to incorporate concepts and
techniques of this program into your daily activities, and
provide a degree of accountability.

PART *I*

ATTITUDE AND SELLING SUCCESS

TWO WAYS TO GO
(Make Your Choice Now)

SUCCESSFUL SALESPEOPLE	UNSUCCESSFUL SALESPEOPLE
Those who maintain a positive attitude.	Individuals who turn negative.
Those who learn and then practice accepted sales techniques.	Those who fail to learn and apply proven selling techniques.
Those who remain positive.	Those who underestimate their future as salespeople.
Salespeople who listen to their prospects.	Those who do all the talking and never learn a customer's needs.
Individuals who know the products they sell.	Salespeople who don't bother learning product features and benefits.
Salespeople who learn to manage their time and set priorities.	Individuals who are more interested in their commissions than their prospects.
Those who consider themselves problem solvers.	Salespeople who refuse to learn from their mistakes.
Those proud to be involved in the selling profession.	

Add your own:

    (in both columns)

The difference between an effective and ineffective salesperson is usually a matter of sensitivity, sincerity, attitude, and selling skills—all of which can be learned.

4

PERSONALITY AND SELLING

Personality obviously plays an important role in the selling process. This is why some people claim that successful salespeople are born and not made. But is personality all that is necessary? Aren't there skills that true professional salespeople use? The answer is yes. Professionals use a wide variety of techniques to approach clients, present products, answer questions, and close sales. Each selling situation requires that these techniques be adapted and skillfully used, but the basics that everyone needs to learn remain the same.

> Case studies help provide insights you may not already possess. Seven case problems are included in this program. Please give them your careful attention.
>
> The case on the opposite page will help you understand the personal value of sales training.

CASE #1:
A DECISION FOR RAMONA

Ramona, now 27 with two children, has decided to enter the labor market. Although she has a friendly nature and dresses with style, Ramona lacks self-confidence and has trouble initiating conversation in social situations. Yesterday Ramona was offered a sales training opportunity in a high-fashion department store. When she talked to her husband about the offer, he downplayed the job. "I think you are attracted to the glamour of working with fancy clothes and not considering how difficult it is to deal with demanding customers. You had good clerical skills at one time, why not brush up on them and look for an office job?"

The following morning Ramona talked the job offer over with her good friend Marci. After hearing Ramona's description, Marci was enthusiastic about the opportunity. "It seems ideal to me, Ramona. You have never been in a situation where you have to meet new people and this job will help you learn to be more outgoing. The job is kind of a personality development school where you will learn to deal effectively with all kinds of people. Since you know clothes, it should be easy. In my view being trained as a professional salesperson will benefit you in your future career choices. The person who offered you the job must see your potential. Go for it!"

    I agree with Ramona's husband. ☐
    I agree with Marci. ☐

Please turn to page 66 and compare your thoughts to those of the author.

IF YOU HAVE CUSTOMER CONTACT, YOU HAVE SELLING OPPORTUNITIES

When you think of professional selling positions in retail stores, insurance and real estate firms, or in direct home selling (Avon calling!) you expect these individuals have received formal sales training. But what about bank tellers, receptionists, supermarket checkers, food servers, hotel clerks, flight attendants, or telephone service representatives? Could they also benefit themselves and their organizations with sales training?

The answer is an unqualified yes. Most employees, whether they recognize it or not, engage to some degree in the selling process. For example, bank tellers and loan officers may not sell tangibles but they have a list of important services to offer customers. Anyone dealing with the public is engaged in customer relations which sells customers on returning to that organization whenever a product or service is needed.

Many of the basic selling techniques used by professional sales people are useful to anyone who has customer contact.

WHAT CAN SUCCESS IN SELLING DO FOR YOU?

In addition to a higher income, learning professional selling techniques can do many *personal* things for you. *Three* of the ten statements below are false. Place a check in the square opposite the false statements, and match your answers with those at the bottom of the page.

☐ 1. Dealing with customers is less exciting than the work involved in most other jobs.

☐ 2. Selling brings out the best in your personality.

☐ 3. Salespeople are made, not born; if you don't plan and work hard, you'll never be exceptional at selling.

☐ 4. Attitude is more important in selling positions than most other jobs.

☐ 5. Those good at selling can often quickly improve their income.

☐ 6. Learning to sell now will help you succeed in *any* job in the future.

☐ 7. In your first sales job, what you learn can be more important than what you earn.

☐ 8. Selling is less demanding than other jobs.

☐ 9. You have less freedom in most selling positions.

☐ 10. A smile uses fewer muscles than a frown.

FALSE STATEMENTS.

1. Most people find selling exciting.
8. Selling is more demanding because you must stay positive all the time.
9. Most selling jobs—especially those outside—provide far more freedom than more confining positions.

> **View your first selling position as an opportunity to test your personality potential.**

YOUR ATTITUDE IS SHOWING

WHAT IS A POSITIVE ATTITUDE?

On the surface, attitude is the way you communicate your mood or disposition to customers or co-workers. When you are optimistic and anticipate successful encounters with others, you transmit a positive attitude and they usually respond favorably. When you are pessimistic and expect the worst, your attitude often is negative and customers will tend to avoid you. Inside your head, where it all starts, attitude is a mind set. IT IS THE WAY YOU LOOK AT THINGS MENTALLY.

Marsha, a college graduate with many talents, is never satisfied with her image, complains a lot about her job, and usually responds to others in a superior manner. She focuses her mind on the negative aspects of her life.

Roberta, a high school graduate, works hard to improve her image, looks for the good things in her job, and responds to others in a positive manner. She focuses her mind on the positive aspects of her life.

Who would you employ as a sales person?

Marsha ☐
Roberta ☐

EXERCISE:
YOUR ATTITUDE TOWARD SELLING

To measure your attitude toward selling, complete this exercise. If you circle a 5, you are saying your attitude could not be better in this area; if you circle a 1, you are saying selling is probably not for you.

	Agree				Disagree
There is nothing demeaning about selling a product or service to a prospect.	5	4	3	2	1
I would be proud to tell friends selling is my career.	5	4	3	2	1
I can approach customers, regardless of age, appearance, or behavior, with a positive attitude.	5	4	3	2	1
On bad days—when nothing goes right—I can still be positive.	5	4	3	2	1
I am enthusiastic about selling.	5	4	3	2	1
Having customers turn me down will not cause me to be negative.	5	4	3	2	1
The idea of selling challenges me.	5	4	3	2	1
I consider selling to be a profession.	5	4	3	2	1
Approaching strangers (customers) is interesting and usually enjoyable.	5	4	3	2	1
I can always find something good in a customer.	5	4	3	2	1

TOTAL

If you scored above 40, you have an excellent attitude toward selling as a profession. If you rated yourself between 25 and 40, you appear to have serious reservations. A rating under 25 indicates another type of job would probably be best for you.

YOU DO NOT NEED
TO BE AN
EXTROVERT TO
BE
SUCCESSFUL AT SELLING.

QUIET,
THOUGHTFUL PEOPLE OFTEN
ARE VERY
SUCCESSFUL.

SELF-CONFIDENCE SCALE

You may have rated high in attitude, but if you do not have the confidence to meet customers, all is lost. This exercise is designed to help you measure your self-confidence. Read the statements and then circle the number you feel best fits you.

	High			Low	
I can convert strangers into friends quickly and easily.	5	4	3	2	1
I can attract and hold the attention of others even when I do not know them.	5	4	3	2	1
I love new situations.	5	4	3	2	1
I'm intrigued with the psychology of meeting and building a good relationship with someone I do not know.	5	4	3	2	1
I would enjoy making a sales presentation to a group of executives.	5	4	3	2	1
When dressed for the occasion, I have great confidence in myself.	5	4	3	2	1
I do not mind using the telephone to make appointments with strangers.	5	4	3	2	1
Others do not intimidate me.	5	4	3	2	1
I enjoy solving problems.	5	4	3	2	1
Most of the time, I feel secure.	5	4	3	2	1

TOTAL

If you scored high on both the attitude and self-confidence exercises, you have a winning combination as far as selling is concerned. If you scored lower on self-confidence than attitude, you are receiving a signal that you need more experience dealing with people. This program can help increase your self-confidence.

CHARACTERISTICS OF SUCCESSFUL SALESPEOPLE

Sometimes quiet, unassuming salespeople become highly successful because they are accepted more easily by customers who resent those more aggressive. At other times salespeople who are more outgoing and verbal are successful because they communicate an immediate warmth that dissipates the psychological barriers some customers have toward being sold something. That is why there are so many different successful models in the field of professional selling. The only characteristic that everyone needs to succeed is a postitive attitude.

Following are ten common personality characteristics found in successful salespeople. Place a plus in the square opposite those traits you already possess, a check mark opposite those you can more fully develop in the future, and a question mark in any remaining squares.

☐ Self-starter
☐ Persistent
☐ Like people
☐ Energetic
☐ Problem solver
☐ Good communicator
☐ Not easily frustrated
☐ Ambitious
☐ Like money
☐ Enjoy recognition
☐ Friendly

CASE #2

CASE #2:
WILL JOE SURVIVE?

Study this situation carefully and decide whether you feel Joe will succeed as a professional salesperson.

Fresh out of college, Joe accepted a high-paying but demanding sales position with enthusiasm. A physical education major, Joe planned to be a high school football coach but could not find a suitable coaching position in the geographical area of his choice; so he turned to sales.

Big, handsome and something of a free spirit, Joe has no fear of people or situations. He speaks up quickly, has considerable self-confidence and is meticulous about his appearance. With his energy and personality, Joe is easy to like. Best of all, Joe does not give up easily. His athletic training taught him that you never give up until the game is over. On top of all this, Joe has natural leadership ability. In his senior year he was, among other things, captain of the defensive football team.

During his two-week sales training, it became obvious that Joe did not always take selling techniques seriously. Somehow, he felt he didn't need to learn how to play the game because his personality would see him through. In group training sessions, and when he was assigned to a professional salesperson to gain experience with live prospects, Joe appeared to be listening. Later, however, when he had an opportunity to demonstrate what he had learned, he relied on his own ideas. In those instances, when Joe was permitted to approach a prospect on his own, he did most of the talking and did not make a serious attempt to understand the prospect's point of view. Despite his poor listening skills, everyone in the firm (especially fellow sales trainees) likes Joe, and many feel he is a natural salesperson. Most predict early success for Joe.

What is your opinion? Will Joe succeed and become a long-term professional? Check the appropriate box below, and compare your decision with that of the author on page 66.

☐ Joe will succeed.
☐ Joe will eventually fail.

14

FIRST IMPRESSIONS
ARE CRITICAL

Because customers have different values and personal standards, some employers encourage their salespeople to communicate a safe or conservative image. Employers in some environments (restaurants) require uniforms, others (sophisticated fashion stores) ask their salespeople to adhere to dress codes. When accepting a new position, it is a good idea to discuss the matter of grooming and image before reporting to work.

Do you agree or disagree with these statements?

The way you dress can help or hurt the image you have of yourself. The better your self-image the more positive you will generally be.

Agree ☐ Disagree ☐

The better you look to yourself the better you will look to customers because you will have more personal confidence.

Agree ☐ Disagree ☐

COMMUNICATING YOUR BEST IMAGE

Like an actor or actress, a person who has customer contact is always on stage. Creating a good first impression is essential. It is also important to understand that there is a direct connection between how you look to yourself and your self-confidence. The better your self-image, the more positive your attitude will be. Please rate yourself on each of the grooming areas presented below. If you circle a 5, you are saying that no improvement is required. If you circle a 1 or 2, you need considerable improvement. Be honest.

	Perfect	Good	Fair	Weak	Poor
Hairstyle, hair and/or beard grooming.	5	4	3	2	1
Personal habits of cleanliness.	5	4	3	2	1
Selection of clothing (appropriate to the situation).	5	4	3	2	1
Clothing color coordination.	5	4	3	2	1
Neatness (shoes shined, clothes clean, well-pressed, etc.).	5	4	3	2	1
General grooming: Do you feel your appearance will reflect professionalism?	5	4	3	2	1

When it comes to appearance, I would rate myself:

☐ Excellent   ☐ Good   ☐ Need Improvement

Most successful salespeople claim that to be sharp mentally you must communicate your best image.

16

SELLING STYLE

Each person new to a selling situation must adapt his or her style to the environment. It is one thing to sell complicated computer systems to a foreign prospect, and something quite different to sell cosmetics to a teenager. Listen to your supervisor. Observe co-workers. Then develop a selling style which best fits your customers, products and services. As you do this, keep in mind that the techniques presented in this book fit comfortably into any style. Also there are some fundamentals that apply universally. You will discover some of these on the facing page.

THE PSYCHOLOGY OF SELLING

Here are some tips (psychological tools of the trade) that should help you demonstrate you are on your way to becoming an effective salesperson.

Make customers feel good about themselves. When you listen respectfully, help clients make a decision and then compliment them for making a good one, you help them feel better about themselves. This creates a better relationship between you and your customer.

Expect to be turned down now and then. The sports phrase ''you can't win them all'' is helpful in selling. Program yourself for some disappointments so you won't dwell on defeat when it occurs.

Acknowledge you don't have all the answers to a complex problem. A professional consultant (and smart salesperson) contributes to a solution by working with the client as a partner, not as a know-it-all.

Turn disappointment into an advantage. When you have a good relationship with a client, even if you don't get the sale, it is possible to open the door to future opportunities. For example, the client may refer you to another prospect or, as often happens, buy from you at a future date.

A bird in the hand is worth ten in the bush. Do not be naive about your selling expectations. A sale has not been made until the money is in the bank. Too many times a new salesperson assumes an order without making certain it is secure.

Organize your time. Most salespeople who experience difficulties do so because they do not prepare a daily plan of action. A disorganized salesperson winds up frustrated, discouraged and with few orders. An organized salesperson enjoys a feeling of accomplishment.

REMAINING POSITIVE IS THE GREATEST CHALLENGE OF SELLING

Selling environments often present "up" and "down" attitude situations. For example, it is usually easy to remain positive during peak hours, days, or seasons when the environment is alive and active. It is more difficult when things are inactive. On top of this, when things are active, customers seem easier to satisfy. During slow periods they seem to demand more. Even bosses and supervisors are more difficult when business activity is low. All of this makes it extremely difficult for any salesperson to maintain a positive attitude over an extended period of time. Some experts claim it is the number one challenge!

ELIMINATING DOWN PERIODS

In life, it is impossible to be "up" all the time. Everyone, including the most successful salespeople, has down days. This exercise assumes three things: (1) You are generally a positive person. (2) There are certain things you can do to remain positive. (3) Becoming aware of them can assist you to remain positive.

The action steps listed below help some people maintain their positive attitudes. After reading the list, select the three you feel will do the most for you.

☐ Engage in physical exercise of some sort.

☐ Give yourself more attainable goals.

☐ Try to take life less seriously.

☐ Share your positive attitude with others.

☐ Take more weekend or "mini" vacations.

☐ Maintain a better balance between work and leisure.

☐ Emphasize your grooming more.

☐ Devote more time seeking inner harmony (go to church, do yoga, or read a good book, etc.).

☐ Do more for others.

☐ Seek out those who can provide positive reinforcement for you.

Others: _____

_____

_____

PART *II*

HOW TO PLAY THE SELLING GAME

SELLING IS LIKE PLAYING BASEBALL
COVER ALL THE BASES AND MAKE A SALE

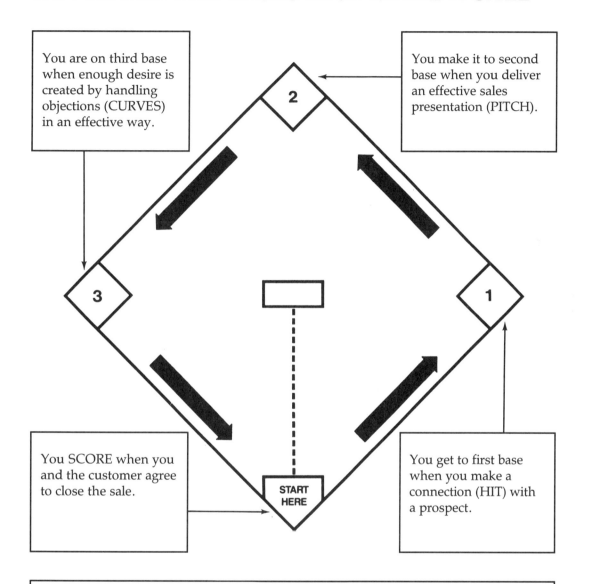

You are on third base when enough desire is created by handling objections (CURVES) in an effective way.

You make it to second base when you deliver an effective sales presentation (PITCH).

You SCORE when you and the customer agree to close the sale.

You get to first base when you make a connection (HIT) with a prospect.

START HERE

SELLING AS A GAME

Professional salespeople like to consider selling as a game for many reasons. You hear them saying: ''Everyday is a new ballgame.'' ''Sometimes you do everything right and still strike out.''

The truth is that playing a ''game'' is more motivating than ''work'' and selling lends itself to the game concept.

You do not need to be a baseball fan for the reference to help you learn the basic selling techniques.

TIPS ON HOW TO GET TO FIRST BASE

MAKE YOUR APPROACH TO THE PROSPECT PROFESSIONAL, PERCEPTIVE, AND POSITIVE.

Note: It is important to qualify a potential customer early. A true prospect is someone who has the need for what you sell, the authority to buy it, and the money to pay for it. It is foolish for you to run around the bases only to be put out at home because you didn't qualify the prospect in the first place.

MOST BATTERS DO NOT GET TO FIRST BASE

If you don't get to first base with a prospective customer, the game is over before it begins. Here are four tips that will help you get off on the right foot with customers.

Send friendly non-verbal signals. A warm smile, solid eye contact, good posture, grooming, and the way you walk are all examples of non-verbal signals. Most important of all is your attitude. When greeting a prospect make sure your non-verbal signals are appropriate before you say anything. Project confidence.

Use a verbal greeting that is sincere, warm, and natural. What you say and how you say it will help both you and your prospect relax. Conversation of a light nature will help break the ice with your prospect.

Demonstrate an immediate desire to help. Act more like a consultant or advisor than a person selling something. This may mean asking questions and listening carefully to what your prospect says. The better the communications now, the easier it will be for you to get to second base later.

Discover customer needs. Unless you discover the needs of a prospect, you can't satisfy them. The effective use of questions will allow prospects to share their problems. If you can help solve the problem, you will probably make the sale. If you can't honestly satisfy any need or solve the problem, say so. Your time, and that of the prospect, is valuable, and your honesty will be respected.

FIRST BASE QUIZ

True	False	
_____	_____	1. Appearance of the salesperson has little to do with getting to first base.
_____	_____	2. Most successful salespeople view selling as a game they like to play.
_____	_____	3. Non-verbal signals are less important than verbal greetings.
_____	_____	4. When you are busy doing other things, a customer is an interruption.
_____	_____	5. As a customer, the attitude of the salesperson often speaks so loudly I cannot hear what she or he says.

ANSWERS: 1. F   2.T   3.F (equally important)   4. F (customers always come first)   5. T

GET TO SECOND BASE: A *PROFESSIONAL* PRESENTATION

KNOW WHAT YOU ARE SELLING

The more you know about the product and/or service your organization provides, the more help you can be to a customer. Those who sell one line of products (computers, stocks and bonds, automobiles) have the advantage of focus. They have the luxury of becoming experts at what they sell.

This concentration is not always possible in other areas. Here are two examples.

(1) Salespeople in retail stores have a wide variety of ever-changing products to sell. Because of this they often must depend upon product labels, co-workers, or even customers for product knowledge.

(2) Banks and Savings and Loan institutions often have dozens of different services for their customers. A branch manager or loan officer often has trouble staying up to date, let alone a teller who must deal first with routine customer transactions. As a result, tellers must learn to understand how to make pleasant transfers to more knowledgeable parties.

USE THE RULE OF THREE

In many retail selling situations, you have the opportunity to present different alternatives of the same product. This is true when selling shoes, clothing, tools, etc. In presenting these kinds of products, show only three varieties at any one time. If you wish to introduce a fourth product, eliminate one already shown. Research has shown that customers do well deciding among three products; however, with more than three confusion sets in. This technique will allow you to begin to close the sale by asking: "Which would you prefer?"

SECOND BASE IS NOT AUTOMATIC

After you are on first base, the prospect should be ready to listen to your sales story. You will, for a time, be in command. Make the most of the opportunity you have earned by following the tips below.

Find the hot button: Different prospects buy the same product or service for different reasons (status, performance, cost, etc.). If you listen carefully, they will tell you what appeals to them. When you discover this ''hot button'' you should be able to steer your presentation more in that direction.

Use visuals: You can communicate better and hold the interest of the prospect longer if you can show as well as tell. If you do not have any formal visuals, a pencil and pad can be effective. You will appear more professional when you do this.

Ask for feedback: It is vital to know if the prospect is listening. Now and then ask questions like—'Does that make sense?' and 'Will that help solve your problem?' To make progress, you must know what the prospect is thinking.

Tell a complete story: If you forget to tell a prospect a key feature about your product or service, you may miss the sale. On the other hand, you don't want to give the prospect more information than is required or desired.

SECOND BASE QUIZ

True	False	
_____	_____	1. Product knowledge does little to give the salesperson additional confidence.
_____	_____	2. The more merchandise you place in front of a customer the better.
_____	_____	3. A ''hot button'' is appealing to a customer's motives for buying.
_____	_____	4. You can't get to second base without knowing the needs or the problems of the customer.
_____	_____	5. It's a good idea to tell the customer everything you know about the product or service you are selling.

ANSWERS: 1. F   2.F (limit to three)   3. T   4. T   5. F (only some of the facts and the benefits)

FACT VS BENEFITS

We all know that an advantage of a polyester shirt is that you can wash it at night and wear it the next morning. No ironing is necessary. In selling such a shirt, polyester is the fact. The benefit is that it saves the customer time and money by drying quickly without wrinkling.

Most customers are more interested in benefits than facts. Talk benefits but keep in mind that the more you know about the products or services the better prepared you will be to answer questions. It is always a good idea to know more about a product than you normally use in a presentation.

CASE #3:
WHO MADE THE SALE?

Although they work for competitive firms, Mary and Sally are equally competent as decorators and each has good sales skills. A few weeks ago both were invited to make a sales presentation to a church committee assigned the task of installing new carpeting in the sanctuary. Over $10,000.00 is budgeted for this job.

Mary takes pride in knowing all of her products, especially carpeting. She reads all available printed materials in addition to asking questions of suppliers. She has visited carpeting mills so she fully understands carpeting construction. During her presentation, Mary stressed the wear factor in the two carpets she recommended, discussed safety factors for senior members, and went into detail on the ease of maintenance. She was prepared to answer any and all questions relative to the advantages and benefits of her carpeting over others on the market. Many questions were asked.

Sally has been content to learn only what she really needs to know about any product she sells. Her concentration is on the psychological benefits of the product on the consumer. She pushes brand names but avoids specifics about the product. In her presentation, she stressed the improved religious atmosphere the carpet would create and the impact the beautiful color would have on church members. Sally is entertaining as well as persuasive in making presentations.

Assume that both Mary and Sally wind up recommending the exact same carpet—same color, same price, same installation arrangements. Who, in your opinion, would make the sale? Place a check in the box of your choice below, and then turn to page 66 to compare your answer with that of the author.

| | Mary would make the sale. | | Sally would make the sale. |

MAKE THE MOVE
TO THIRD BASE

AVOID ASKING PREMATURE QUESTIONS

Once you have qualified a prospect by asking investigative questions in a nice way, it is usually best to wait for additional questions or objections to come from the customer. The primary reason for this is that questions from a prospect are easier to deal with. For example, if you ask a customer how much she/he is prepared to pay for your product, you may eliminate it from consideration before you have had a chance to communicate its value. If you ask what color coat your prospect is interested in, you might have trouble finding the color requested. Why not give yourself the advantage by waiting for such questions to come from the customer naturally?

SELLING IS A PROBLEM-SOLVING PROCESS

Customers buy products and services to solve their problems or enhance their position. Always try to view the problem (or opportunity) as the prospect sees it. Acting as a consultant instead of a salesperson will put you in a position to communicate better, because your insights will provide reasons your product or service can help solve the problem.

WELCOME QUESTIONS

Most customers decide to buy by asking questions. How you answer these questions will determine whether you get to third base or become stranded on second. Here are four suggestions.

Encourage and welcome all questions. The moment you become defensive about your product or service is the moment you lose the game. Listen carefully to each question (or objection) before you start to answer it.

Honest answers, please. Customers will not buy if they have doubts about the quality of a product. If your product has a disadvantage, first acknowledge it and then compensate by pointing out an advantage that outweighs the disadvantage. A product or a service need not be perfect for the prospect to buy. It only needs to be a solution for the customer.

Explain why new is better than old. Here you become more of a teacher than a salesperson. Make comparisons; demonstrate why performance will improve; show how the prospect will come out ahead with your product.

Introduce the Mutual Reward Theory. Explain that in any sound sales transaction, both parties should benefit. Remind prospects that you could not expect any future purchases from them unless they come out ahead now. When the prospect realizes you are sincere, you will finally be on third base.

THIRD BASE QUIZ

True	False	
_____	_____	1. Selling is best viewed as problem solving.
_____	_____	2. A product or service need not be perfect for the customer to buy.
_____	_____	3. Introducing the Mutual Reward Theory into the transaction shows dishonesty.
_____	_____	4. The primary objective of getting to third base is to satisfactorily answer all questions from the customer.
_____	_____	5. Asking clients how much they are willing to pay for a product or service is a smart move.

ANSWERS: 1. T 2. T 3. F (it demonstrates openness and honesty)
4. T 5. F (it is best to demonstrate value and let the question originate with the client.)

BUILDING A CLIENTELE

An excellent policy to follow in selling is to make the sale but treat the customer in such a way that she or he will return to you, and the organization you represent, in the future. To make a sale but alienate the customer is counter-productive in the long run. *Customer satisfaction is a must!* To see that this happens it is important that the salesperson lead customers to make their own decisions based upon their legitimate needs and ability to pay.

CASE #4:
WHO WILL BE MOST SUCCESSFUL?

Jill and David work for a bank where they are in a position to sell customers on various investments such as Certificates of Deposits, Treasury Bills, Tax Free Bonds, Annuities and other securities. Both are new to their jobs.

Jill has a soft approach to clients. When on second base she is most patient in explaining the advantages and disadvantages of each option. When she moves to third base she always tells customers to invest only in those securities within their comfort zone. When she invites questions, she listens carefully and narrows the options down to two or three and encourages them to make a choice.

David follows a similar pattern but when he has patiently answered all questions, he makes a specific recommendation. That is, after carefully evaluating the clients' financial goals, David says something like this: ''Mrs. Jones, it is my opinion that the purchase of tax free bonds would be the best investment for you.''

Who do you feel will be the most successful?

_____

_____

_____

_____

See page 66 for author's comments.

YOU CAN'T WIN WITHOUT CLOSING

By the time you and the prospect get to third base, you have probably invested considerable time and energy. All this is lost if you don't score (i.e. land the sale). There is something very fulfilling when you win. Winning may not be everything as some coaches say (in selling you want a satisfied customer), but it is the primary reward of any professional salesperson.

GETTING HOME SAFELY

GETTING HOME: HOW TO CLOSE A SALE

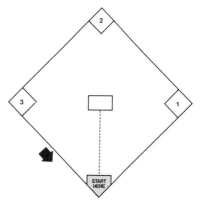

Many baseball teams could have made it to the World Series if they had not stranded so many base runners. Many failures in selling could have been avoided if the salesperson learned how to close a sale. Have confidence in the progress you made getting to third base, but make sure you get home by following with these actions.

Summarize advantages. Frequently, at the end of the selling process, the prospect needs to see all the advantages in one, clear, concise package. This summary makes a ''yes'' decision much easier.

Introduce financial arrangements. You can close a sale by finalizing financial arrangements. When the customer agrees to a financial plan, the sale is usually consummated.

Use a powerful closing statement. Sometimes a single sentence will get you home safely. For example, you might say: ''It appears you have found the best solution to your problem. Why delay?''

Ask for the order. Do it in your own way, but under no conditions should you hesitate to ask the prospect to buy. The fact that you covered the first three bases · gives you the right to make a play for home plate. If you need additional confidence, consider that getting stranded on third may hurt the prospect as much, or more, than it will hurt you.

HOME BASE QUIZ

True	False	
_____	_____	1. Making a sale can be as exciting as scoring a winning run in a ball game.
_____	_____	2. Summarizing the good points of a product previously covered makes it easier for the customer to make a positive decision.
_____	_____	3. It demonstrates poor taste to ask for an order.
_____	_____	4. Some people who find the best possible product or service to meet a need will not buy unless they are sold.
_____	_____	5. Weak salespeople often needlessly leave customers unhappy and stranded on third base.

ANSWERS: 1. T   2. T   3. F (if handled in a sensitive manner, asking for an order is a smart move) 4. T   5. T

HOW *MUCH* PERSUASION?

- Some prospects will
  back away if they
  feel pressured

- Some prospects will
  not buy unless
  they are sold

CASE #5

CASE #5:
WHO CLOSED THE SALE?

Please assume in dealing with this case that the following three factors exist:

Factor 1   Both Sara and Marlow are equally successful salespeople with similar experience. Both work on a commission basis and the sale in question would mean a great deal of money to the winner.

Factor 2   Although they work for different firms, they are selling basically the same product at the same price. Other conditions are similar.

Factor 3   Sara and Marlow have done equally well getting the same prospect to third base. The winner will be the person who does the best job closing the sale.

In her closing, Sara summarized what she said to get the prospect to third base. She stressed the reliability of her product and the reputation of her company. She insured her prospect understood that the product will be delivered on schedule. Sara went so far as to commit herself to train employees who would use the product after it was installed. Sara's closing sentence to the prospect was: "If you give me the order, both you and your firm will be beneficiaries."

Marlow, in his attempt to close the sale, used a different approach. He zeroed in on the problem of the prospect. He indicated that the prospect's organization would continue to lose money until a solution had been reached. His voice slowly increased in volume as he built to a climax designed to win him an immediate "yes." Marlow's closing sentence was: "I'm convinced you have found the best answer to your problem with my product. May I have your order?"

Who, in your opinion, would have closed the sale? Place a check in the box of your choice below and then turn to page 66 to compare your answer with that of the author.

☐ Sara closed the sale.   ☐ Marlow closed the sale.

☐ Both Sara and Marlow closed the sale.

SUMMARY

BEFORE YOU CONTINUE, TAKE A MINUTE TO MAKE SURE YOU HAVE THE BASIC STEPS OF SELLING DOWN PAT.

PROVE YOU KNOW
THE BASICS — REVIEW

In the weeks ahead, keep the comparison between baseball and selling in your mind. Make a serious attempt to fully cover all four bases in each transaction. To help you do this, please write out (in your own words) the missing technique for each base. Once you have done your best, return to the pages indicated to match your answers.

THIRD BASE techniques
(Page 30)

1. Encourage questions and objections.
2. Honest answers, please.
3. _____
4. Introduce the Mutual Reward Theory.

SECOND BASE techniques
(Page 26)

1. Locate and press the hot button.
2. _____
   _____
3. Ask for feedback.
4. Tell the complete story.

GETTING HOME techniques
(Page 35)

1. Summarize advantages.
2. Introduce financial arrangements.
3. Use a powerful closing sentence.
4. _____
   _____

FIRST BASE techniques
(Page 24)

1. Send friendly non-verbal signals.
2. Use a verbal greeting that is sincere, warm, and natural.
3. Demonstrate a desire to help.
4. _____
   _____

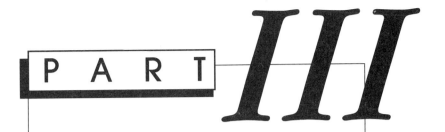

PART *III*

BACK TO BASICS

SOME THOUGHTS ON SELLING IN TOUGH TIMES

1. Experts claim that professional salespeople welcome periods of economic downturn because they know that average and below average salespeople will become discouraged and seek non-selling positions. This shake-out process leaves the field to the "pros" who often increase their incomes during such periods.

2. The expression "when things get tough, the tough get going" applies more to selling than other jobs. When there are fewer customers and competition from other firms becomes greater, successful salespeople become more valuable to their firms and receive more recognition and rewards.

3. It is recognized among selling professionals that an ethical, experienced, and competent salesperson who is willing to work can easily move from one organization to another and, therefore, is never out of a good job.

4. Highly skillful salespeople who use proven sales techniques outsell others by a large margin. Thus one salesperson, paid on a commission basis, can earn three times as much as another in the same position.

5. An individual who learns to sell in difficult times will have a permanent edge on those who learn to sell in easier times. Why? Because they will have more confidence in what they can do.

6. Learning to sell at any time will increase one's ability to communicate and enhance his or her personality. Many people who switched to other professions admit that the basic selling training they received early in their lives gave them a personal advantage they would not have otherwise enjoyed.

LITTLE THINGS COUNT

As this edition of Sales Training Basics is being completed, much of the world economy is slowing down and sales training is becoming increasingly important. Listed below are some "little things" that signal this return to basics.

Read the following ideas. Place a check in those boxes where you agree with the statement.

☐   1. Once a sale has been consummated, it is best to thank the customer and move along to your next activity.

☐   2. It is more difficult to replace a customer than to keep one satisfied.

☐   3. Never make a promise to a customer unless you and your organization will be able to keep it.

☐   4. Always endeavor to radiate confidence in yourself and in your products and/or services.

☐   5. An excellent way to handle a disappointment is to forget it and go right back to work.

☐   6. A salesperson should not criticize or condemn competitors.

☐   7. A salesperson should show respect for the opinions of a customer.

☐   8. It is usually a good idea to let customers feel that an idea you introduced belongs to them.

☐   9. Even when customers are wrong, they should be treated with sensitivity.

☐   10. Nothing can take the place of a smile.

☐   11. The moment that selling becomes work (instead of a game) a person becomes less effective.

☐   12. Often your attitude speaks more loudly to customers than anything you say.

EMPLOYERS ARE ALWAYS LOOKING FOR QUALIFIED SALESPEOPLE

RELATED SELLING

In many selling situations (such as retailing), once a customer decides to buy she/he becomes a good prospect for additional sales.

Some products go together.

Paint, brush, thinner,
drop cloth, etc.

Coat, shirt, tie, etc.

Lipstick, eye shadow, powder, etc.

Hamburger, french fries.

Personal computer, software, printer,
supplies, etc.

In these situations, the salesperson does the customer a favor by suggesting related items which might save an extra shopping trip or make the original purchase more usable.

BECOME AN EXPERT AT RELATED SELLING!

LITTLE COURTESIES COUNT BIG

It is noticeable in almost all organizations that serve the needs of customers that a few salespeople measurably outdistance the performance of others. Why is this? It usually narrows down to a few special things that high performance salespeople do for people they serve that others fail to do. What are these secret treatments?

On the opposite page you will find eight ways professional salespeople build what is often called a "personal trade." A personal trade consists of customers who prefer the service of one salesperson (waitress, bank teller, retail store salesperson) over that of others. They often ask to be served by a certain person or wait in line until the salesperson they seek is free to serve them.

Please read each of the eight "special treatment" secrets and then prioritize the list by placing the number 1 in the box you prefer over all others and continue through the list. Place the number 8 in the box opposite the treatment that is least impressive to you.

EIGHT SECRETS TO SUCCESS

CUSTOMER SPECIAL
TREATMENT EXERCISE

1. ☐ FOLLOWING UP AFTER A SALE. In some cases it is a smart move to contact the customer a few days after a sale has been made. For example, if you sell an appliance like a refrigerator to a customer you might follow up with a telephone call to verify that the delivery was made on time and that everything is working to the customer's satisfaction.

2. ☐ REMEMBERING CLIENTS' NAMES AND SOMETHING PERSONAL ABOUT THEM THAT YOU DISCOVERED DURING THE PREVIOUS MEETING. People almost always enjoy *personal* attention and treatment and when they receive it once they usually return to the same organization and salesperson again and again.

3. ☐ MAKING GRACEFUL EXCHANGES OF MERCHANDISE. Sometimes, despite the best efforts of a salesperson, a customer winds up with the wrong item and brings it back. When such a customer and the returned merchandise are warmly welcomed back and a suitable exchange is facilitated, any guilt the customer might have had about returning the item is erased and a long-term relationship is created.

4. ☐ COMPLIMENTING THE CLIENT. Everyone likes to receive a sincere compliment now and then. Salespeople who learn the skill of paying compliments that are sincere and deserved increase the number of clients who return to them for service.

5. ☐ HELPING THE CUSTOMER SELECT WHAT IS RIGHT FOR THEM WITHOUT PRESSURE. When you guide a customer to a selection that makes them happy they recognize you as a professional and they are often willing to wait in line to receive your help again.

6. ☐ PROVIDING SPECIAL TREATMENT TO ALL CUSTOMERS, NOT JUST A FEW. Showing preferential treatment to one customer is often noticed and resented by others. All customers deserve *equal* consideration. In other words, you build a personal following by giving special assistance to *everybody*.

7. ☐ PROJECT YOUR MOST COMFORTABLE, NON-IRRITATING VOICE. Usually, a quiet, modulated voice is most appreciated by customers . . . especially when the transaction is one that is confidential in nature.

8. ☐ COMMUNICATING A SENSE OF HUMOR. Customers desire to make a sales transaction as enjoyable as possible. When they leave feeling better than when they arrive, you can anticipate their return.

SELLING VIA THE TELEPHONE

In the future, more and more selling will be done via the telephone. This is called telemarketing. The reason it will occur is because making personal sales calls is becoming increasingly expensive.

This suggests that whenever possible you should use the telephone and use it effectively.

PROFESSIONAL SALESPEOPLE HAVE ALWAYS USED THE TELEPHONE TO KEEP IN TOUCH WITH KEY CUSTOMERS.

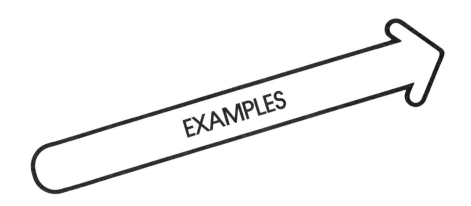

EXAMPLES

TELEPHONE OPPORTUNITIES
(Let your fingers make you successful)

| Hazel |
Hazel is the number one salesperson in the appliance department. When she is not on the floor with a customer you will find her on the telephone talking to prospects or keeping in touch with previous customers. For example, she makes a practice of contacting customers who have just made a purchase to make sure the installation was made on time and that everything is working right. Other salespeople in her department do not bother to do this. Hazel made this statement when presented with an award recently: "I'm not a better salesperson than the others, I just use the telephone as a partner or second salesperson to build better relationships."

| Ramon |
Ramon is an outside salesperson representing a sporting goods wholesaler. His territory is the entire state of Arizona. Last year, to cut down on travel expenses, Ramon got permission from his customers to call on them every four months instead of every two. To compensate, he promised to telephone them once each month to take orders, make suggestions, and handle problems. As a result, Ramon has increased sales 20%, cut travel expenses 40%, and now spends more time at home with his family. To the amazement of his sales manager, customers seem as satisfied as previously.

| Genelle |
Genelle sells a line of cosmetics to drug chains and large department stores. She is most effective with sophisticated cosmetic buyers and on scheduled days does make-up demonstrations for customers. Genelle's only problem is that taking care of key accounts gives her little time to contact smaller drug stores, family department stores, and other retailers who could profit from her line. As a result of careful analysis, Genelle discovered that her most ineffective day in working the key accounts was Monday. On an experimental basis, she decided to stay home each Monday and use the telephone to contact smaller accounts. In doing this, she worked out a telephone presentation that allowed her to cover all four bases. Also, she would always thank the prospect for permitting her to make a telephone instead of a personal contact. After perfecting her telephone presentation, Genelle was able to increase sales by 15% without neglecting any key accounts.

HOW TO BE A
TELEPHONE PROFESSIONAL

(It's not as easy as you think)

Two major factors are involved in successful telephone marketing or selling. First, you are dependent upon the tone and quality of your voice to communicate a positive, friendly attitude that will get you to first base. Second, your introductory remarks are critical because you do not have the advantage of eye contact and smiling with potential customers.

Most experts recommend you introduce yourself by name, state the organization you represent, and if possible, use the name of a third party to get you started. The idea is to create interest and intrigue about yourself and the purpose of your call.

To improve your telephone approach, you might consider experimenting on a home message recorder (your own or one belonging to a friend). Prepare your introductory remarks ahead of time, make the call and deliver your message. Then listen to your message and react to your voice as though you were the potential customer.

DOING A NUMBER ON THE TELEPHONE

Successful salespeople make better use of the telephone than people in almost any other profession. The following exercise should measurably improve your telephone techniques by helping you discover what you may be doing wrong. Circle the appropriate response. Further instructions are provided at the bottom of the page.

HOW OFTEN DO YOU:	NEVER	SELDOM	SOME-TIMES	OFTEN	ALWAYS	IMPROVE-MENT NEEDED
Think about calling a prospect but fail to do so.	1	2	3	4	5	☐
Put a smile into your voice as you pick up the receiver.	5	4	3	2	1	☐
Fail to return a client call.	1	2	3	4	5	☐
Communicate a positive attitude.	5	4	3	2	1	☐
Sound annoyed when you answer a call.	1	2	3	4	5	☐
Solicit customer feedback by telephone.	1	2	3	4	5	☐
Accomplish the same results by phone as you would from a personal call.	5	4	3	2	1	☐
Save travel time through effective use of the telephone.	1	2	3	4	5	☐
Cover all four bases by telephone in a professional manner.	5	4	3	2	1	☐
End the conversation with a pleasant, upbeat comment after summarizing the reasons for the call.	5	4	3	2	1	☐

If you circled a 3, 4, or 5, your selling telephone techniques need improvement. Check those squares in the right hand column where you are serious about making improvements.

HOW TO HANDLE
THE DIFFICULT CUSTOMER

Listed below are ten ways to react to an over-demanding or otherwise hostile customer. ONLY FOUR ARE ACCEPTABLE FORMS OF BEHAVIOR. Place a check in the box opposite those you believe to be acceptable and match your opinions with those at the bottom of the page.

☐　1.　Show slight disgust on your face so the customer will know you consider him or her a problem.

☐　2.　Challenge the customer with your eyes.

☐　3.　Let the customer talk through his or her anger.

☐　4.　Consider the customer in an objective manner; refuse to take negative comments personally.

☐　5.　Listen with your eyes.

☐　6.　Become distant and less communicative.

☐　7.　Disarm customer by asking: ''Are you trying to give me a problem?''

☐　8.　Start to whistle.

☐　9.　Send back the kind of behavior you are receiving.

☐　10.　Immediately steel yourself with a pleasant smile and say to yourself: ''I'll show everyone I can handle this customer in such a way she will want to return to us for service in the future.''

Acceptable responses: 3, 4, 5, and 10

TEN UNFORGIVEABLE MISTAKES

(Check those you intend to avoid.)

1. ☐ Failure to carefully plan each selling day ahead of time.

2. ☐ Waiting for someone else to motivate you.

3. ☐ Failure to develop a strategy which will cover all four bases with qualified prospects.

4. ☐ Giving up too soon on a qualified prospect.

5. ☐ Refusing to take advantage of an opportunity to close the sale.

6. ☐ Failure to maintain good relations with key customers before you lose them.

7. ☐ Forgetting to follow up after a sale has been made.

8. ☐ Refusing to maintain a positive, personal image.

9. ☐ Failure to learn from mistakes.

10. ☐ Neglecting to maintain a positive attitude.

SELLING OCCUPATIONS PAY OFF IN MANY WAYS

It stands to reason that not everyone can be happy in a selling position. Many people are happier in a multitude of other roles. It also makes sense that if an individual is not happy in a selling job they will not be good at it.

Can you force yourself to be happy in a selling role?

No, but the only way you will know is if you give it your best shot over a reasonable period of time. Many people with negative views of a selling career discover that with a few behavioral changes they can enjoy the process and be successful. Some discover that selling brings out the best in their personalities and they prefer selling to all other occupations for which they qualify.

CASE #6

CASE #6:
WENDY THE WAITRESS

All waitresses and waiters receive the same basic wage at the restaurant where Wendy works, but she takes home almost twice as much as the others because of the additional tips she receives. This happens because Wendy gives everyone special treatment and, as a result, customers ask for her by name and her tables are occupied more than those of others. In addition, she has a quiet, fun way of selling the better wines and desserts. Naturally, customers tip more when their bills are higher.

Andre, a new waiter who previously worked for an exclusive dinner house where he was trained in the tradition of formal service, has become friendly with Wendy. "Wendy," he said, "I really envy your style as a waitress. Everybody loves you and you out-tip me at least two to one. Before I lost my previous job because they priced themselves out of business, I had an income similar to you. Do you think that I can shed my formal ways, learn to be openly friendly and patient like you, and double my tips?"

"Sure you can, Andre, and I will give you all the help I can."

Even with Wendy's guidance, will Andre be able to change his style as a waiter? Will he be able to double his current tip income?

_____

_____

_____

Turn to page 67 to match your thoughts with those of the author.

SELLING AND
TIME MANAGEMENT

As a salesperson you will have considerable freedom. How you control this freedom is up to you. Failure to manage your time is an easy way to end a selling career.

CASE #7

CASE #7:
WHO WILL WIN THE TRIP TO HAWAII?

Susan and Eddie occupy identical sales positions with the same firm. A contest is underway, and because of their excellent sales records, both Susan and Eddie are in a good position to win first prize: a trip to Hawaii. The contest will end in three months.

Susan and Eddie are outstanding in using professional selling techniques. Both cover all four bases with ease. But Susan is unbeatable when it comes to personality, initial contacts, and getting customers to like her. Susan feeds on her own success, and her enthusiasm is catching. There is one problem, however. Susan has a tendency to burn out after a few weeks. Somehow, after a highly successful selling period, she falls apart for awhile. Some of this may be because she wears herself out physically, but most of it occurs because she doesn't plan ahead and organize her time on a daily, sustainable basis. Susan works more on impulse than strategy; enthusiasm than logic. When she is in tune, she is fantastic; but when Susan has down periods, it takes her time to climb back.

Eddie is the opposite. Although he does not enjoy peak selling periods like Susan, Eddie is always in charge of himself. He plans every day ahead of time and sets priorities methodically. Eddie makes the best possible use of his time because he always knows what he is going to do next. He is known among his co-workers as ''Steady Eddie'' and is highly respected as a professional salesperson. Eddie is measurably better at keeping old customers happy than Susan.

Will Susan win the trip to Hawaii or will Eddie?

Which individual do you feel has the best chance?

☐ I vote for Susan.   ☐ I vote for Eddie.

Compare your selection with that of the author on page 67.

58

YOU'LL BECOME MORE PROFESSIONAL IF YOUR MANAGER ESTABLISHES HIGH STANDARDS AND HELPS YOU TO REACH THEM THROUGH TRAINING AND ENCOURAGEMENT.

Most sales supervisors or managers started out knowing little about the selling process. They reached their present positions because they developed and applied many skills. As a result, they know that you, too, can be successful selling. In some cases they will insist that you learn and apply skills that *they* have found successful. In other cases, they will let you develop your *own* style. The fact that these managers have high expectations for you is good. If you welcome this attitude on their part you will become a professional salesperson sooner.

SELF-MOTIVATING IDEAS

REWARD YOURSELF

Getting a hit, stealing a base, and scoring a run in a baseball game are rewarding. In selling, the ultimate reward is making the sale. Those who are successful in doing this often motivate themselves with a series of personal rewards they create ahead of time. Below are some rewards you might find motivating. Keep in mind that such rewards should be enjoyed *after* you accomplish some of your goals.

Daily Rewards

Going to a health spa at the end of the day.

Dining at a favorite restaurant.

Spending time with a special person.

Other:_____

_____

Weekly Rewards

Going for a week-end trip.

Attending a concert or sporting event.

Other:_____

_____

Monthly Rewards

Taking a "mini-vacation".

Making a special purchase.

Other:_____

_____

Annual Rewards

Achieving special recognition for your sales performance.

Taking a special trip such as foreign travel.

Other:_____

_____

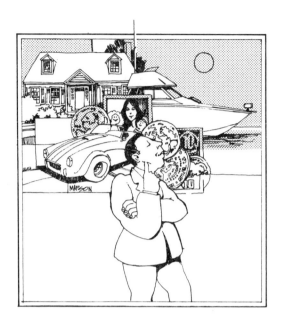

MOST PEOPLE GIVE UP SELLING CAREERS
BECAUSE THEY BECOME DISCOURAGED—NOT
BECAUSE THEY LACK THE SKILLS TO SUCCEED.

THE FORMULA ON THE NEXT PAGE WILL ACT
AS A REMINDER TO HELP YOU SUCCEED DURING
THE DAYS AHEAD. YOU MAY WISH TO ATTACH
IT TO YOUR REFRIGERATOR OR BATHROOM
MIRROR.

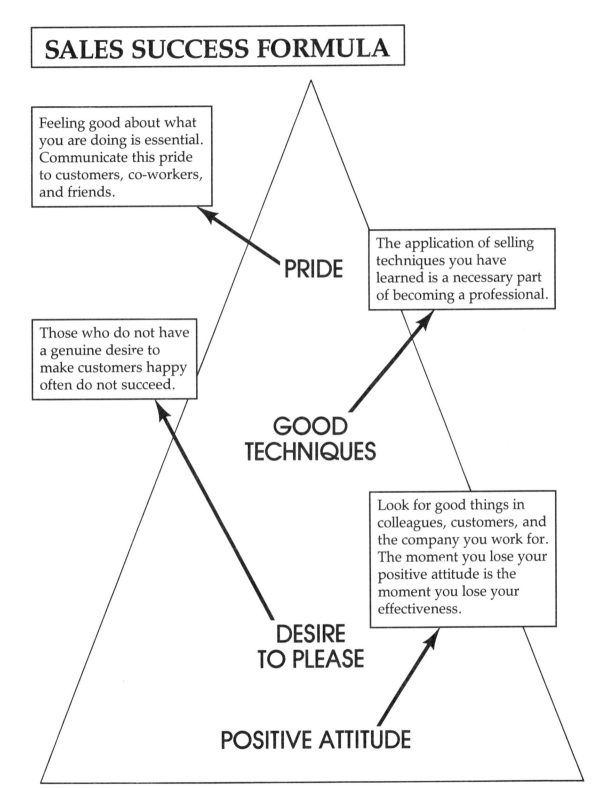

SALES SUCCESS FORMULA

Feeling good about what you are doing is essential. Communicate this pride to customers, co-workers, and friends.

PRIDE

The application of selling techniques you have learned is a necessary part of becoming a professional.

Those who do not have a genuine desire to make customers happy often do not succeed.

GOOD TECHNIQUES

Look for good things in colleagues, customers, and the company you work for. The moment you lose your positive attitude is the moment you lose your effectiveness.

DESIRE TO PLEASE

POSITIVE ATTITUDE

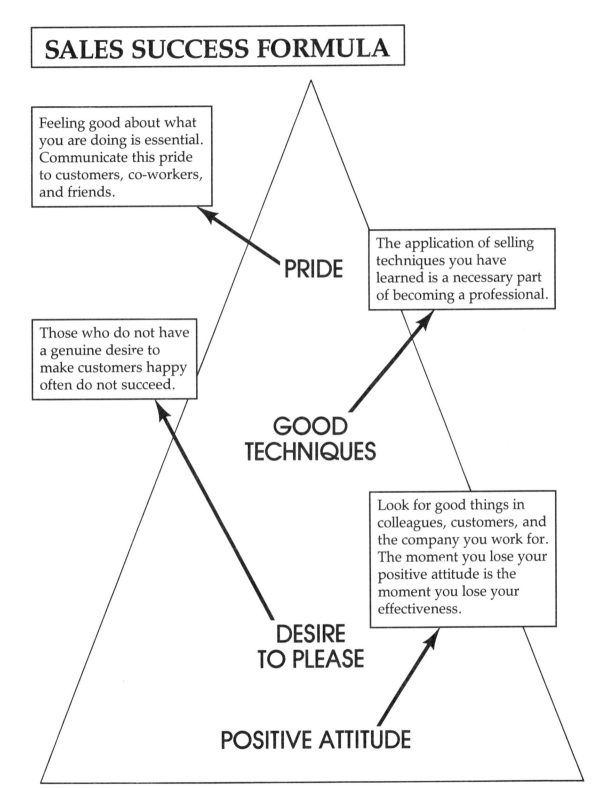

62

IT IS TIME TO MEASURE THE PROGRESS YOU HAVE MADE. ON THE FOLLOWING PAGE ARE 20 STATEMENTS WHICH ARE EITHER TRUE OR FALSE. EACH IS WORTH 5 POINTS. ANSWERS WILL BE FOUND ON THE PAGE FOLLOWING THE TEST.

SCORE YOURSELF

EXERCISE:
DEMONSTRATE YOUR PROGRESS

For each statement below, put a check under true or false.

True   *False*

_____ _____   1.   Financial institutions do not need to teach their people selling techniques.

_____ _____   2.   There are more successes than failures in selling.

_____ _____   3.   Without a positive attitude, good sales techniques are useless.

_____ _____   4.   Quiet people, even those with great confidence, are seldom successful at selling.

_____ _____   5.   Salespeople who view themselves as consultants have a psychological edge over others.

_____ _____   6.   Comparing selling to baseball emphasizes the point that selling is a process rather than a single event.

_____ _____   7.   The best place to discover a prospect's needs is toward the end of the sales pitch.

_____ _____   8.   Most customers are more interested in facts than benefits.

_____ _____   9.   The best way to keep a customer happy is to practice the Mutual Reward Theory.

_____ _____   10.   A professional salesperson should never ask for an order.

_____ _____   11.   Grooming plays a minor role in communicating a good image.

_____ _____   12.   A skillful salesperson always attempts to make customers feel better about themselves.

_____ _____   13.   When customers raise objections, it usually means they have begun to make up their minds.

_____ _____   14.   Related selling is when you suggest other items that complement the one already sold.

_____ _____   15.   Professional salespeople rely on in-person calls and disdain the use of the telephone.

_____ _____   16.   It is more difficult to keep an old customer than to find a new one.

_____ _____   17.   Learning selling techniques in a retail store can improve one's career in all areas.

_____ _____   18.   The way to become a professional salesperson is to analyze mistakes and then make behavioral changes so you don't repeat the same mistake.

_____ _____   19.   Closing the sale is the easiest part of selling.

_____ _____   20.   A positive attitude plus good sales techniques constitutes the best possible formula for selling success.

[ ]   TOTAL   Turn page for answers.

ANSWERS TO EXERCISE ON PAGE 63

1. **F** More and more banks are teaching selling techniques.
2. **F** Countless people have tried selling and turned to other careers.
3. **T** A negative attitude will turn a customer away even if the salesperson uses good techniques.
4. **F** Quiet, sensitive salespeople can be extremely successful.
5. **T** This is true because they listen better and are more in tune with the problem of the customer.
6. **T** All steps are important, but it is the way the process is put together that makes the difference.
7. **F** Third base is too late in the process; first base is the right answer.
8. **F** Although customers appreciate some facts, they are more interested in what the product or service will do for them.
9. **T** When both the customer and the salesperson come out ahead (the purpose of the Mutual Reward Theory), the relationship continues.
10. **F** Asking for the order at the right time is highly professional.
11. **F** Grooming plays a major role because sometimes a salesperson does not get a second chance to make a good impression.
12. **T** If you make someone feel better about him or herself you have strengthened your relationship with that person.
13. **T** That is why all objections should be encouraged.
14. **T** Suggesting additional products is the sign of a good salesperson.
15. **F** Professional salespeople make maximum use of the telephone to save time and money.
16. **T** This is especially true if the customer has been neglected.
17. **T** Successful executives often start out as salespeople.
18. **T** Self-analysis is critical after each selling experience.
19. **F** The most difficult part of the selling process is the close.
20. **T** The combination of a positive attitude and good techniques is unbeatable if the welfare of the customer is realized.

LOOKING AHEAD

CONGRATULATIONS! Your score indicates the progress you have made in a short period of time.

How can you become increasingly successful? Here are 5 tips.

1. Review this material often.

2. Apply several of the concepts in this book immediately as you work.

3. Discuss your selling experiences with your manager to better evaluate your progress by using the Voluntary Contract on page v.

4. Order and read other self-help books listed on page 69 such as *Personal Time Management, Attitude: Your Most Priceless Possession, Successful Self-Management* and *Quality Customer Service.*

5. Practice, practice, practice!

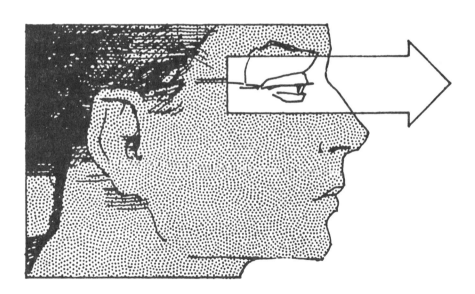

AUTHOR'S SUGGESTED ANSWERS

Case #1

A Decision For Ramona. Sales training can be a great confidence builder and personality "booster." Should Ramona take advantage of the sales training and become a professional, she will enhance her future in all directions.

Case #2

Will Joe Survive? It is the opinion of the author that Joe will fail unless he learns to take selling seriously. Personality alone is not enough. In fact, soft-spoken, well-organized salespeople, who are good listeners, usually outsell those who rely excessively on their personality. Joe seems to feel selling is a piece of cake. Until he accepts it as a profession requiring self-discipline, his chances of survival are poor.

Case #3

Who Made The Sale? Although it could go either way, the author would give the edge to Mary because of her deeper product knowledge and the fact that committee members seemed more involved in her presentation. The more one knows about a product, the more confidence that person has in selling it. This probably came through more during Mary's presentation than in Sally's. In spending other people's money, the committee members would probably lean toward the salesperson who stressed long-wear qualities and could back that claim up with facts.

Case #4

Who Will Be Most Successful? It should be a close race, but Jill should come out ahead because she leads her clients to a decision and then lets them make it. David, on the other hand, plays the role of the "expert" and is, in effect, making the decision for the client. A professional salesperson (consultant) helps a customer make the right decision but the customer still makes it. It is doubtful whether either Jill or David have been in their jobs long enough to be considered "experts" on financial matters.

Case #5

Who Closed The Sale? Although both Sara and Marlow may close the sale, the author supports Marlow. Reasons: (1) The problem-solving approach is often more effective. (2) Building up to a climax, if not overdone, can swing a normal prospect in your direction. (3) Marlow's closing sentence is more powerful and stands a chance of getting an immediate "yes." Sara's closing sentence gives the prospect an opportunity to retreat. For those who may feel Marlow's close contained too much pressure, the reader is reminded that getting to third base was a big investment in time and effort. Providing the bases were covered well, a strong close would be in order.

Case #6

Wendy The Waitress. Becoming a more personal and friendly waiter will be more difficult for Andre than Wendy suspects. After one has been trained and has been successful with one style it is not always "natural" for one to behave in a different manner. Andre needs to adapt to the more informal working environment and talk more in a friendly way with customers, but he should do it his way. Perhaps a "blend" of his formal style with a new approach would be best. It is also true that some customers will appreciate Andre's more formal style than will others. There is no reason why he can't measurably increase his "financial income."

Case #7

Who Will Win The Trip To Hawaii? It will be a close race, but the author votes for Eddie because organization usually pays off in the long run. Susan will have trouble maintaining her enthusiasm over a three-month period while Eddie will probably show greater consistency. If Susan eliminated her down-periods, she could be a runaway winner.

FINAL REMINDER!

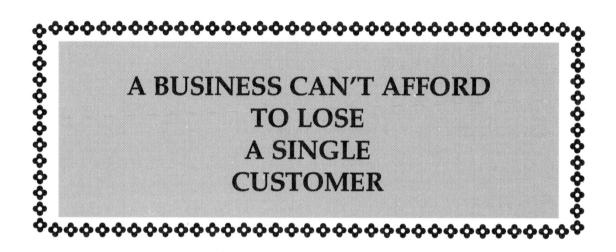

**A BUSINESS CAN'T AFFORD
TO LOSE
A SINGLE
CUSTOMER**

NOTES

NOTES

OVER 150 BOOKS AND 35 VIDEOS AVAILABLE IN THE 50-MINUTE SERIES

We hope you enjoyed this book. If so, we have good news for you. This title is part of the best-selling *50-MINUTE*™ *Series* of books. All *Series* books are similar in size and identical in price. Many are supported with training videos.

To order *50-MINUTE* Books and Videos or request a free catalog, contact your local distributor or Crisp Publications, Inc., 1200 Hamilton Court, Menlo Park, CA 94025. Our toll-free number is (800) 442-7477.

50-Minute Series Books and Videos Subject Areas . . .

Management
Training
Human Resources
Customer Service and Sales Training
Communications
Small Business and Financial Planning
Creativity
Personal Development
Wellness
Adult Literacy and Learning
Career, Retirement and Life Planning

Other titles available from Crisp Publications in these categories

Crisp Computer Series
The Crisp Small Business & Entrepreneurship Series
Quick Read Series
Management
Personal Development
Retirement Planning